Praise for *Upriver*

"What excites me about Carolyn Kremers' *Upriver*: Just when you think you know where a particular poem has parachuted you into the vast terrain we call Alaska, everything shifts: foreground, background, attitude, mood, generation, gender, language and custom, a vast landscape and history deeply violated, deeply loved. Alaska herself—a sometimes cruel, ever-demanding shape-shifting region—feeds, inhabits and haunts these pages... This beautiful book—snow-packed, melting, thick with time, spiritualized with dashes of rhyme and dollops of dance and prayer—reads like a lyric break-through memoir of open and often discomforting discovery and brave self-revelation."

—Al Young, former poet laureate of California and author of *Coastal Nights and Inland Afternoons*

"A few writers are fortunate enough to discover a place that nurtures them and gives their work depth and meaning. It could be a bench of land above a river or something as seemingly insignificant as the way light can illuminate a favorite desk, a place that beckons them to write. A smaller number seem to be able to capture the very spirit of a place. Carolyn Kremers is one of those rare writers and her place is Alaska's Yukon-Kuskokwim Delta and its people and to a lesser extent Fairbanks where she now lives. Somehow she has crossed the gulf that often separates people from people, language from language, culture from culture. This book is a roadmap to the heart of Alaska by a writer who has earned our attention."

—Tom Sexton, former poet laureate of Alaska and author of *I Think Again of Those Ancient Chinese Poets*

"How seemingly simple are the poems in *Upriver*, yet how profound; how dreamlike, yet how charged with reality, immediately and firmly grounded in the earth and human experience. The themes of this poetry are basic and multifaceted, the voice rich and resonant. I thank Carolyn Kremers for bringing this world, her world, in this way, in these words, to all of us."

—Pattiann Rogers, recipient of the Lannan Literary
Award for Poetry and author of *Wayfare*

"*Upriver* takes place in two distinct regions of Alaska—the Y-K Delta and the Interior. I'm not aware of any other book of poems that takes on life in these two very different parts of Alaska. These poems show glimpses of a woman making her way in territory that's nourishing and dangerous, harsh and achingly beautiful."

—Peggy Shumaker, current writer laureate of
Alaska and author of *Gnawed Bones*

upriver

upriver

Carolyn Kremers

university of alaska press
fairbanks

University of Alaska Press
P.O. Box 756240
Fairbanks, AK 99775-6240

ISBN 978-1-60223-202-0

Library of Congress Cataloging-in-Publication Data

Kremers, Carolyn, 1951–
Upriver / Carolyn Kremers.
    p. cm.
ISBN 978-1-60223-202-0 (pbk. : acid-free paper) — ISBN 978-1-
60223-203-7 (electronic)
1. Alaska—Poetry. I. Title.
PS3611.R465U67 2013
811'.6—dc23
                                2012032608

This publication was printed on acid-free paper that meets the mini-
mum requirements for ANSI / NISO Z39.48–1992 (R2002) (Perma-
nence of Paper for Printed Library Materials).

Cover design: Dixon Jones
Cover art: *Kongakut River* © Ursula Schneider
Interior design: Taya Kitaysky

Printed in the United States

For my sister,
Nancy Kremers

contents

Tununak

The Interior

Shapeshifting

Return to the Y-K Delta

Fairbanks

Storyknife

Tununak, Alaska

I'm sitting on the edge of Hilda's bed, and she is dying: Hilda, my beloved neighbor, whose language—like that of all the other elders here—is Yup'ik...

Now I am looking out the tightly closed window, and listening. Hilda is asleep and I am awake. My tears come.

So this is where we are, at this moment, on this hurling ball of rock and time. There they are, the Pretend People, looking down on us every day, Hilda, every day in this closed-up room, and looking out over the sea, looking backward and forward and down inside me, every day, even when I am not here. Even when I think I am alone.

So this is where we are.

The heads of the Pretend People cut sharply against the blue sky. Far up the treeless hill, they seem small, attentive, ancient as the wind.

A V of white-headed emperor geese flies over.

Then there is nothing in the frame of glass but the green tundra and the hill, clean sky, and that pile of rugged rocks.

—*Place of the Pretend People: Gifts from a Yup'ik Eskimo Village* (1996)

After some people read my first book,
they wanted to know
what happened next.

They asked if I was going to write
a sequel. I said I didn't know,
but it turned out the next book

was this—a book of poems—
and yes, I guess it is
a sequel. Only nobody reads poems anymore,

the critics say.
Well, I have witnessed evidence
to the contrary.

Storyknife.
A Yup'ik Eskimo storyknife
was usually made from wood, bone, or ivory

by a father, uncle, or grandfather
for a young girl in the family.
Boys rarely used storyknives (people say),

but sometimes they listened and watched.
The handle of the storyknife
was often carved as a bird, an animal, or fish

and the blade decorated with a circle-and-dot motif
or other symbolic, repeated designs. Sometimes
the storyknife was just a wooden stick.

Later, metal butter knives were used
or metal strips from packing crates.
The girl used the storyknife to draw pictures

in a "smoothened" patch of mud, wet sand, or snow,
as she told a story to herself or to friends.
Sometimes also, songs were sung.

The story might be a myth, a tale,
or a story of the girl's own...
Here, then, is a story,

a continuing, sky/human story. Already
it is slipping in the wind—

Walrus ivory storyknife from Southwest Alaska with animal design on handle, circle-and-dot motif, and many decorative lines. Length: 17.6 cm (6.93 inches). Collected circa 1920s or 1930s by John and Lulu Heron.

Courtesy of the University of Alaska Museum of the North. Catalog number 0638-6042. Photographer: Barry J. McWayne.

Additional information about the poems may be found at the back of the book in notes.

I am without money again this spring, but somehow the material will be found: a few boards and nails, some paint and tar. When the boat is built, I must find a new place to fish, perhaps upriver at the mouth of Tenderfoot. Last fall I watched the eddy there; it was deep and slow.

—John Haines, *The Stars, the Snow, the Fire*

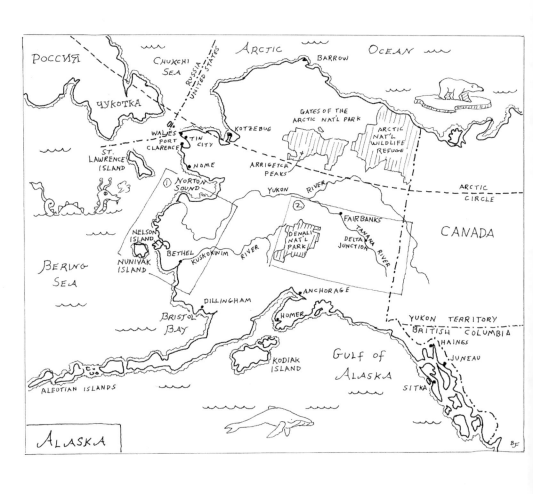

РОССИЯ

ЧУКОТКА

CHUKCHI SEA

ARCTIC OCEAN

BARROW

GATES OF THE ARCTIC NAT'L PARK

ARCTIC NAT'L WILDLIFE REFUGE

KOTZEBUE

RUSSIA / UNITED STATES

WALES
PORT CLARENCE
TIN CITY

NOME

ST. LAWRENCE ISLAND

ARRIGETCH PEAKS

① NORTON SOUND

YUKON RIVER

ARCTIC CIRCLE

CANADA

②

FAIRBANKS

DENALI NAT'L PARK

DELTA JUNCTION

TANANA RIVER

NELSON ISLAND

BETHEL

KUSKOKWIM RIVER

NUNIVAK ISLAND

BERING SEA

DILLINGHAM

BRISTOL BAY

ANCHORAGE

HOMER

YUKON TERRITORY

BRITISH COLUMBIA

HAINES

JUNEAU

SITKA

KODIAK ISLAND

GULF of ALASKA

ALEUTIAN ISLANDS

ALASKA

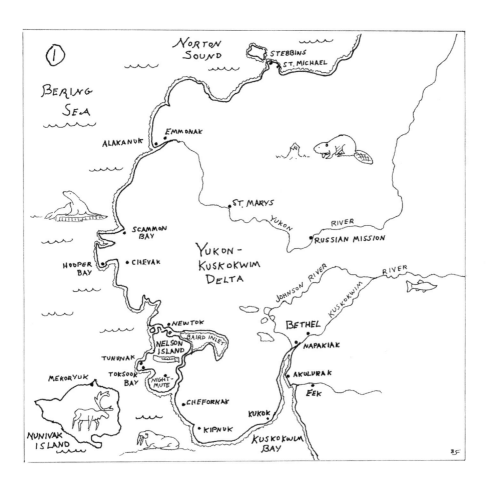

① NORTON SOUND

BERING SEA

STEBBINS
ST. MICHAEL

ALAKANUK

EMMONAK

SCAMMON BAY

HOOPER BAY

CHEVAK

ST. MARYS

YUKON   RIVER

RUSSIAN MISSION

YUKON-KUSKOKWIM DELTA

JOHNSON RIVER

KUSKOKWIM   RIVER

BETHEL

NAPAKIAK

NEWTOK

BAIRD INLET

NELSON ISLAND

TUNUNAK

TOKSOOK BAY

NIGHT-MUTE

MEKORYUK

CHEFORNAK

AKULURAK

EEK

KUKOK

KIPNUK

NUNIVAK ISLAND

KUSKOKWIM BAY

B5

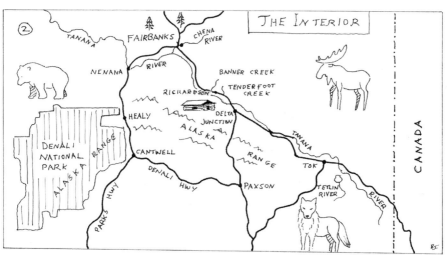

② THE INTERIOR

TANANA

FAIRBANKS

CHENA RIVER

NENANA

RIVER

BANNER CREEK

RICHARDSON

TENDERFOOT CREEK

HEALY

DELTA JUNCTION

ALASKA

DENALI NATIONAL PARK

ALASKA RANGE

CANTWELL

DENALI HWY

PARKS HWY

TANANA

RANGE

TOK

PAXSON

TETLIN RIVER

RIVER

CANADA

B5

Tununak

Two girls storyknifing. Tununak, 1973.

Photographer: Lynn Ager Wallen.

Sestina Kyrie

She has never seen a real shaman,
but Mark says his grandmother was one,
and isn't it true that God
lives inside everything, even or especially (Lord have mercy)
inside a shaman? Christ have mercy. Piece
of bread, sip of wine, "God bless you all," says the priest.

Once a Presbyterian, neither has she known, before, a real priest.
A shaman
might be more exotic, but she likes the peace
inside this balding man, the one
who tells a joke right next to her at dinner with friends
    and then says, laughing, "Mercy,
yes, I'll have another piece of turkey. Praise God."

Everywhere, she hears *Ellam Yua.*
    "Owner of the weather, spirit of the universe." God.
Not just inside the dusty wooden church
    but over the whole, wild island that priests
used to tackle by dog team, Lord have mercy,
Christ have mercy. She can hear the island, like a shaman,
talking, especially when the priest and everyone—
elder, student, mother, father, wiggling fur-wreathed child—
    extends a hand and murmurs, "Peace."

Something about that word, "Peace,"
electrifies fingers and, God,
it shoots up her bundled arm into the one
place that no person, not even a priest,

can really know or understand, a buried, shaman place,
Lord have mercy,

Christ have mercy.
And there's a peace
that reaches in, circles around, settles down,
shaman-like, as if there were a God.
The priest
blesses purple and yellow dyed tundra grass baskets,
    and people give

one dollar bills or quarters
    (when she remembers, she brings quarters, Lord have mercy).
Women in new calico *qaspeqs* sing an offering
    with that unpeaceful, screeching, scraping, shaman sound
heard in all God's Eskimo churches,
a screech she loves, doesn't imitate.
Slowly, with a Yup'ik echo, the priest
reminds everyone God is Love, God is Light, God is One.
    Which She is,

and anyone
who has felt the rhythm (Lord have mercy, Christ have mercy)
and the power and the glory, with or without a priest,
of peace,
goodwill toward men, and women, knows that God was inside
Mark's grandmother. And She is a real shaman.

The New Teacher

We forget our pencils and lose our pens,
but she won't share. She lives alone
in Todd's old house, where there's ghosts
and very many mouses.

"Don't you be scared? Don't you be
lonely up there?" But she says no.
She don't have no TV and she don't eat meat,
but she gets salmons from Sally

and cuts them slow with a knife.
So slow. She's strict. Sometimes
she yells at us—she talks reeally fast—
but she can play guitar. And piano,

too. She plays organ
at the church and makes all the elders
smile. She plays LOUD, with no mistakes.
And the choir sings good.

"Why you never wear no makeup?"
"Why you never wear no dress?"
"Do you got a boyfriend? Do you got a baby?"
"Why you got two pillows on your bed?"

She's fun to visit, 'cause her house is empty,
not crowded, and it smells like hot chocolate
(coconut lotion, she says)
and she got a real mirror, not a metal one

like at the school. She gives us erble tea
with honey, and she has a very lot of pictures
we can look at, of us. She plays our rock tapes
if we bring them, Metallica and Motley Crüe.

Some people see her in the post office,
they feel shy, but she smiles big.
And when she out walking, everybody knows
it's her, even in blizzards, even in fog

or at night with no moon,
because of her long, blue legs.

The New Students

To her they smell comfortable,
like fish, sweat, sleep—
or like soap, fresh
from the laundromat, where showers

cost six quarters. The little ones
grab her arms and legs
with sticky hands, take her "downtown,"
skipping, pull ropes for water,

call out whose house
is whose. They walk on ice, not scared,
reveal sod ruins and a skull, yes, watching,
yellow, almost whole.

Boys offer soft black puppies,
girls braid her hair.
"Will you skate with us?"
"Will you be back next year?"

They want to know everything.

She cannot tell them.
Instead, she asks for words.
Agayuvik, they say, pleased. Church.
Elitnaurvik, school. *Kalikat,* book.

Aqumi, sit down. *Tengssuun,* plane.
Nayiq, ringed seal. *Usuuq!* Watch out!

Akutaq, Eskimo ice cream.
Anaq, dog poop. "And humans', too."

"I like you," she says.
Assikamken, they answer, suddenly shy.

They bring wildflowers, fossils, white
rocks, leave them on the steps
when she's not there. When she is,
they swing the chain inside the door, bing

the kitchen timer, want to know
what spices are for, and insurance.
They chew snuff and spit it, grinning
at her tales of cancer and mouths.

Some eat popcorn with chopsticks,
watch *2001* in school,
and she tries to explain
that the apes are not real,

what a synthesizer is,
how it feels to ride a horse,
or pet one.
They laugh lots.

She learns
to speak slowly,
not use big words,
watch their eyebrows,

try to listen.
There is too much to hear.
"Don't touch me, bitch!"
Marjorie hisses,

eyes burning through the desk,
long black hair. Pregnant,
like a bomb. Not wanting to give up—
"Happy birthday, Marge"—

one day she comes home from school
and smells a ghost:
cigarette smoke
inside the arctic entryway.

This girl could set the house on fire.
Or does she want to talk?

Eskimo Dancing/*Yurarluni*

Cut and paste from the *Yup'ik Eskimo Grammar* book

Yugtun qantuten-qaa?
Do you speak Yup'ik?

Yurarcit ciin?
Why are you dancing?

Yurarciigaliukut.
We are no longer able to Eskimo dance.

Yuraryuumirtua.
I yearn to Eskimo dance.

Yuranguq.
He is starting to dance.

Yurartuq yuut iliit.
One of their people is dancing.

Yurartu'rtuq.
He keeps on dancing.

Yurartuq arnaq-llu.
The woman is also dancing.

Yurartut yuut ilait.
Some of the people are dancing.

Kass'aq kituuga?
Who is the white person?

Yurartuq kass'aq Yup'igtun.
The white person is dancing like an Eskimo.

Taringenguq.
She is starting to understand.

Ellangenguq.
She is beginning to see.

Yuraryugngaunga.
I can Eskimo dance.

Yurartua.
I am dancing.

Neqtangqertuq kuim paingani.
There are fish at the mouth of the river.

Ancient Comb

—At Port Clarence

Annie somersaults on my bed,
crows, in wet socks and a red
Kool-Aid mustache.
"Her real mother
has been drinking again,"
Rebecca, her grandmother, says.
"Even the tents are not happy.
That green mold grows,
eats canvas."

Summer of drizzle and fog.
Sixty splayed salmon rot on the racks.

Rebecca laughs
like sunlight, remembers:
one night last August,
digging in the mounds,
she found an ancient
ivory comb.

"Only two teeth missing."

Dr. Seuss & the Department of Fish & Game

It could be a dolphin, it could be a seal,
it could be a mussel, enough for a meal.
It could be a musk ox, perhaps it's a moose,
or a migrating white-throated emperor goose.
It could be a walrus without any head,
raped for its ivory then dumped with the dead
   like a sack.

      How strange
      to think paper could stretch
      to fit everyone, when some
      animals give themselves up
      to the hunter, and others
      are slaughtered like cows.

      Bright eyes, dark faces
      spark in the Eskimo school.

      "What's a hormone?"
      "Additive?"
      "Twenty-six pounds of grain—what's that mean?"
      "Why can't you eat meat?"
                     I just don't,
      usually, except wild, when
      (*Quyana!*)

it could be a beaver, it could be a tail,
it could be a two-ton bowhead whale.

It could be a reindeer, perhaps it's a grouse,
or a caribou grilled in a prefab house.
Or it could be a carcass of blubber and bones,
a meal for the grizzly whose deep tracks groan,
  melting in the sand.

What Scares Me

I pull on mukluks
for the first time since
moving away
and I get frightened.
I can't remember her name.
Burrowing through long
furry leggings lined
with scraps of *qaspeqs*—
dark green, violet, burgundy
dresses, ribboned, rick-racked—
my feet touch bottom
and nestle
against thick felt,
matted tundra grass
and two thousand years,
stiff sealskin soles
tanned in the cold
to make them white.

"You are a giant,"
the mascara-ed girl translates,
giggling, as her grandmother stoops
to measure my foot
along a line of linoleum,
wraps string
around my muscled calf, loops
a knot, her curved back barely
high as my knees.

I draw bright red
and dark blue yarn
too tightly
around the tall red tops,
crinkling fine rows
of red, white, black beads stitched
with cracked
and glittered fingers
in painstaking
ones, twos, threes.

"Red is for good luck,"
they tell me together
wind stampeding
oil stove sweating
smell of reindeer stew.

Fumbling with moosehide
ankle ties, I forget
to cross them twice.
Empty palms smooth
coarse black wolverine
soft brown beaver belly
rugged spotted seal, feeling
for relatives, trying
to trigger her name.
Josiah, Edward, Matthew, John,
Ellen, Martha, Chauntelle...

"I'm wearing spirits on my feet,"
I want to tell the talking white people
that night as they eye
so much fur. But I can't get
enough air. The live mukluks
and I flee
out of town
to the bending forest.

"Kituusit?"

"Susan.
Susan Thomas."

The Language Keepers

For Bob Hooper (1915–2005)

Angyarpaliyugngayugnarquq.
He can probably make a large boat.

September.
Amirairvik.
Time of shedding velvet.

October.
Qaariitaarvik.
Time of masked festivals.

November.
Cauyarvik.
Time of drumming.

December.
Uivik.
Time of going around.

January.
Iralull'er.
The bad month.

February.
Kanruyauciq.
Time of frost.

March.
Kepnerciq.
Time of cutting seals.

April.
Tengmiirvik.
Geese coming.

May.
Kayangut Anutiit.
Coming of eggs.

June.
Kaugun.
Hitting of fish.

July.
Ingun.
Molting of birds.

August.
Tengun.
Flight of birds...

Blooded moon
and new ice shiver
in the northeast wind.

Black-turned night
drapes sleep
over everything except

the trumpeter swans

    tilting,
    bright,
    in the one great circle.

The Interior

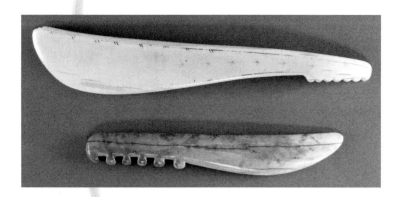

Two storyknives.

Top: Curved walrus ivory storyknife from Southwest Alaska. Green and red lines, circle-and-dot motif, repeated short, double marks on blade. Six knobs carved along bottom of handle. Length: 23.5 cm (9.25 inches). Collected between 1937 and 1965 by William and Rhoda Thomas.

Bottom: Fossilized walrus ivory storyknife from Nelson Island. Six knobs carved along bottom of handle. Circle-and-dot motif on top rim. Length: 17.8 cm (7.01 inches). Collected before 1945 by Frank Waskey.

Courtesy of the University of Alaska Museum of the North.
Catalog number (top): UA67-098-0048.
Catalog number (bottom): 0301-0002.

Photographer: Angela J. Linn with Kirsten Olson.

Trapline

Tin airtight stove
and stretched visqueen beckon,
seventy miles from the road,
and she's hungry.
Dangled two days off the back
of the sled, she's hungry
enough to eat a hot dog: her first
in fifteen years.
He pries four from the rock-
hard package cached outside
on a spruce branch, tucks them
into boiling macaroni water.
When they swell like shaved
pink poodles, she chases them around
and around, dicing up buttons that wiggle
in slippery yellow cheese sauce.
Sitting on milk crates, they savor
the peppery, nitrate dogs.

Long after tea, he reaches up
to light the lantern, opens the door:

white clouds pile in and, humming,
she dumps soapy warm water
out of the pot, under the night,
under loping chartreuse light.

At the Tetlin River

She moans at your approach,
white breath crowding
around her like a coat

and I follow, needing
her rufous beauty,
not wanting it captured but wanting

to witness your ability
to feel and not feel. Your blue strength. Free
in this forest, you press her neck firmly

under your arm, and I see
your face, not cold, hear all her air
forced out in a wheeze, released

with the pain in her paw, out the ends of her long black-tipped hair.
When she is still, you hand me the body,
knowing I must touch it to share

the warmth slipping oddly
from her fur into you, like a pact.
I lay the red fox gently

on the snow where she'll soon freeze whole,
and you reset the trap
she stumbled into, meant for wolves.

Backcountry Unit #12

Thirty-eight caribou spill over a ridge and run down the mountain, cross a snowfield, drop into the canyon, splash across Sunrise Creek. They bound up the other side, your side.

A golden eagle tilts in the sun, white tail feathers, pterodactyl wings. Body and spirit spiral up and up and up in an updraft, up and out of range of your binoculars into a blueness you can feel on your face, smell in the blue cool mornings through the mosquito-screened tent.

You are sleeping, walking, cooking in grizzly bear country, and you are loving it. Fresh holes gape in the damp tundra where arctic ground squirrel tunnels have been ripped to roots, huge dirt clods thrown back in a frenzy of paws and claws. The grizzly rarely wins this race, but there will be others. She can run forty miles an hour. You rehearse how to stand your ground, how to face her if she charges. You would think of someone you love or of music. Intricate. And loud.

Denali National Park, once called McKinley, founded in 1917. No one has died here by a grizzly. Twenty maulings, but no one has died. These bears have not learned to associate backpackers with food, and you do not intend to teach them. You cook a hundred yards from your tent, stow raisins and toothpaste in a three-pound bear-proof canister a hundred yards from your kitchen, wash the scent of rice from your hands and face before sleeping. You scan every ridge and willow patch for bears, blonde bears, ravaging, ravishing, thick-furred bears.

Piles of hardening brown scat dot a snowfield. Near Sunrise Glacier, a long hole in the tundra gleams white with sheep hairs, fresh earth scattered all around. Is this a wolf cache, robbed by a bear? Yesterday? Today? Footprints, footprints. Dall sheep, caribou, arctic ground squirrel, fox.

You watch a caribou calf through binoculars, marvel at how the herd clatters down the mountain, over snow, through rushing water, sweeping the spindly calf with it. You search the hillside, see no sign of why they spooked.

A single loon floats in a beaver pond, guarding its mate and an egg. Thumb-sized ptarmigan chicks hop in the grass. This is the day after Solstice. Night never falls. Tiny pink moss campion flowers glow on green cushions, fluorescent pink, fluorescent green.

You will camp in this country for three days, wake every morning to creekwater music; to concerts of snowbirds, robins, Lapland longspurs; to a necklace of snow gracing green jagged mountains. Cradled in the singing, in a large life cycle, a deep picture, you will forget that you could fall prey to a startling brown blur more decimating than any accident or disease in a civilized place.

These things will stick, they will go back with you. And leaving little trace, you will take all that you can.

All I Wanted

All I wanted, my love,
was every night to lie
(every light-tossed night)
in your arms, like mist, like glass
about to break, like a bell high
enough to be heard above
the trees. All I wanted was for you
to stroke my hair when I cried,
to hear you listen, and be able to say,
yes, I do.

Kass'aq with Nunivak Mask

aloud—

Looking

(female)

She wished she could
look at him
more directly, turn and look
at him. But his eyes
ran deep, bordered with tracks:
black brant, king eider, crane.

That night—
guest in his home,
seeing the hand-carved masks—
she knew. He could smell dried fish, hear
old ice, remember people
in the Delta, dancing

(male)

(dancing, remember
people in the Delta
dancing, remember
dancing).

(female)

Some mornings on waking,
she feels him
roll over her. Without thinking,
she is in his eyes, looking
and he
is a breaking blue river.

Dancing

(female)

He sleeps.
Light breaks.
She waits, quietly,
to open the door,
enter his room, ask
to wake one morning
in his eyes.

(male)

Fat loon fishes.
Old man carves.
(Something starves.) Gladly
bend red willow, soar,
enter feathers, mask
to make whole: dancing
eyes.

alternating—

(female)
(male)

He sleeps.
Fat loon fishes.
Light breaks.
Old man carves.
She waits, quietly
(something starves),
to open the door, gladly
bend red willow, soar,
enter his room, ask

feathers, mask
to wake (to make)
one morning
whole dancing
in his
eyes.

simultaneously—

(female)   He sleeps.   (male)   Fat loon fishes.
               Light breaks.   Old man carves.
               She waits, quietly,   Something starves.
                                                Gladly
               to open the door,   bend red willow, soar,
               enter his room, ask   enter feathers, mask
               to wake one morning   to make whole: dancing
               in his eyes.   eyes.

What I Did Not Imagine

I imagined a light-haired woman
who fit under your arm
like a child, like a friend
who knew how to laugh
at anything, how to hold you
in her eyes, color of clarity.
She was delicate-boned,
practical, you said, with two feet planted

on the ground. You said
her needs were simple
and her desires, but I did not believe
any woman's needs were simple,
and I knew, if only in my imagination
and my fear, that her desires
were not simple, either.

To desire you was to wish
for rich white clouds, green
ground, thunder
and the slash of lightning,
close; how a robin sings
when the storm stops
and the air is new
like promises. Once

there was a morning
for smoothing the furrow
in your brow, seining an inlet

of silver, but the net
got tangled
and something inside
is screaming
still
screaming

Apparition

When this heat comes,
it will be a thick
sweet Georgia heat
and someone

will lie with him,
windows wide
open, sticky, slipping.
He will come, inside,

to a ghost
seated on a bed, frozen
night, two hands pressed
around stoneware—

>   how the glaze
>   transfers heat and human contact,
>   how hard the clay;

>   how the lights begin,
>   green and pale,
>   and a woman sees them,

>   still,

in Georgia
shine dancing.

Before You Go

give back my body

give back my ecstasy
fingers trailed

down my nakedness
like an electric filament
turning on and off and on

give back my courage
the thrill in my belly

when I felt how it might be
to let you
seed a child and

give back my wish
to not grow grey and crooked

without hands
to hold and be stroked by
oh, window, eye of wind

Shapeshifting

Two boys with storyknife drawings. Umkumiut fish camp, Nelson Island, 1976.

Photographer: James H. Barker.

Two with Spears

I.

No one else has said
her gaze is like a peregrine's.
Startled, she sees again
the ragged pass at Arrigetch,

the sudden bird, silent, steady,
coming deep from fog, coming
at eye-level. Feather breast. Grey-white-
grey-white-grey. Seated now

at the crowded lunch table,
she wants to kiss the neck
so big and bare beside her.
Hot room. His throat smooth

in a cool green jacket.
She cannot look,
needs not to want to glide
over him, like a peregrine,

suddenly soft
and near in fog.

II.

He asks to visit. Walking,
she wants to touch
palms, line up lifelines,
press his pulse to hers.

His fingers, by her side,
seem small. She looks away.
When at last he takes her
hand on this fall morning,

brown earth touches
a pale moon. If he had learned
to walrus hunt, she might feel
calluses, but he lives

in two worlds. The white one
claims his hands. She asks
his Iñupiat name, delights
in the story: how his namesake

killed nine polar bears,
two with spears. He asks
if he might take her shooting,
wants to show her why he switched

from a rifle to a pistol. A moose
must get very close, he says, so close
you can look into its eyes
as it gives itself up.

III.

Like the jagged peaks at Arrigetch
and clear sky, they touch
with awestruck fingers.
Even mistranslated,

the Athabascan name stuns.
Awestruck, outstretched.
Outstretched, awestruck.
He wraps his hunger

around the legs he says can reach
another time zone. She sucks
his small fingers, lets them play
between her teeth. She remembers

looking down from a Cessna
over tundra more wide
and green than she had ever seen,
how it lay sprinkled with white dots

like daisies, like unpainted
Easter eggs. Swans,
nesting tundra swans.
Sometimes they unfurled

their hundred elegant wings in a freedom stretch
that, later, she feared
she might not know again.
Is this how it happens?

Beyond the window,
another snow flies.
After years and broken glass,
is this how it happens?

Peregrine, Moose, Raven, Swan.
Polar Bear, Walrus, Bearded Seal.
Peregrine, Moose, Raven, Swan.
Polar Bear, Walrus, Bearded Seal.

IV.

He says his daughter
has chicken pox, misses evenings
with Dad, the way they usually
walk around the block

to Pasta Bella's for dessert.
He tells how he asks for *espresso*
and the machine whirrs, while his hazel-eyed
child swings her legs and orders

cheesecake with blueberries.
"Store-bought blueberries," she says,
and grins. "Real ones
are better." He tells her

what he did in school that day,
she tells him, and sometimes
they trade jokes. "Oh, Dad,"
she says, "you're so silly."

He says she worried she'd miss
Halloween, but she got well
enough to walk a few blocks in the paws
of a cat with a long black tail.

His wife's friend from Kotzebue
stitched it. And last year
in Ohio, when this little person
who means everything to him

was in second grade, she said,
"I know what, Dad.
Let's go as Eskimos."
So they did.

V.

This is the night the moose comes:
deep holes, long scuffs
in the snow. A full moon lights
the long domed veil

and she knows.
She will never leave.
When she goes, if she does, something
will stay. He says white people

think they know the future.
They live by calendars
in their heads. He laughs.
He tells how his uncle

taught him to steady the trigger
and the seal. "Live now,"
his uncle said, in Iñupiaq.
"Look now."

VI.

"Did you put out food
for the moose?" he asks,
lying fully clothed on her bed.
She laughs. She likes to talk

with him this way.
"I could never do that,"
she says, "unless the moose
was starving." She knows better

than to feed wild animals.
"I wouldn't want to make
a moose a pet." His eyes settle
on the distance. "My father

used to ride the back
of a polar bear," he says. "Kids
in the village took turns. My father says,
even now, he remembers

how it felt to jump up and grab the fur—
'Hang on!'—while the bear
flopped on its belly and slid
downhill like a pancake.

A hunter had shot
the bear's mother, not knowing
she had a cub. When he saw,
he took it home.

One day, an Air Force officer
from Tin City came
to Wales. He saw the half-grown cub
and shot it, just like that."

VII.

They will find the beach
that she has always wanted
to visit, he says, and they will walk it,
looking for what has washed up.

She knows
that whatever he discovers,
he will give to her, or to someone,
because he gives away

everything. He says
he'd like to see her
in the long white dress,
the sleeveless cotton dress,

that she has always wanted
to wear on that beach,
barefooted, toes teasing
turquoise water. They will walk

a long time, he says,
breeze ruffling her silvered hair,
until Raven flings them
down into sand and up

into wide, wide sky.

Return to the
Y-K Delta

Women and children in the village of Akulurak, circa 1920s. Girl in center holds a storyknife.

Courtesy of Jesuit Oregon Province Archives. Akulurak Mission Collection. Catalog number: 153.8.01a.
Photographer: Unknown.

Bethel at Christmas

Like the moon, full as a heart
of new and old friends,
we encircle
the Christmas tree,

Yup'iks and *kass'aqs*
drinking boxed wine
in this "damp" town,
Mamterillermiut,

where every drop of liquor
is hand-carried or home-brewed.
Some sip sodas, coffee, or tea,
some the pale pink plash,

and talk touches health aides
on call night and day, villages
the size of thumbnails, a favorite
place you go to pick blueberries

"in fall time" and marvel
that so-and-so met so-and-so
in Hawaii, how people
are different, how snow creaks

under skis, and tundra
in the full moon looks
like desert, like white sand,
sagebrush, tumbleweeds.

The snow gives in the dark
its sudden hills,
and you glide without thought
or lover, rabbit fur hat

blocking wind. Later
at the Christmas party,
someone tells of skiing
the bluffs toward Napakiak.

Take a left turn
and there will be dog teams
stringing the horizon,
a sudden moment

of hugging and knowing, yes,
we change in this riverine town,
swallowed by sky, willow bushes
taller than human heads,

an occasional spruce and,
there, the Christmas party
house built with logs
that drifted downriver,

each with a story
we will never know,
can only imagine and smile,
saying yes, it was a good

evening, yes, we should do this
more often, yes, forty mile gusts
may keep us from running
the 12K tomorrow, day of the mink festival.

Come Sunday, homemade cookies
for sale at the high school,
five dollars a pound.
Piano recital with friends,

the wind picking up,
cherise sundown,
colored lights in the foam dome's
star-shaped window, *tua-i-llu*

give thanks
for this glory
of night and season,
this heart full

of ache and peace,
this place.

The Shortest Distance

He is letting her
hug him (or is she
letting herself?)
hug him harder
and with more grace
than she has ever plumbed.
He is turning
to night
and Georgia,
and she is letting
him turn.

This moment
comes back in spring,
in the back row
of a B.A.G. play
about a man
who wears a wig
and a chicken costume, is dying
of cancer and knows
how to laugh
at everything, how to laugh
and laugh and laugh
and let things

be. How long
will she remember
this embrace?
How long will she insist
that the shortest distance
between two points
is a synapse?

Freak Warm Weather

Scarlet jacket,
earphones, tunes;
wide eyes blue as birds
or water. He says he
works with child victims
of beating, incest, alcohol.
Tundra Women's Coalition.

How does he
do it? How does he meet
this cold, flat place, straight
out of college and Syracuse,
New York—muscled arms,
green heart, Jesuit
volunteer—and make it

through? February
in Bethel, almost March.   *Daylight*
Freak warm weather.
I picture him last year
playing rugby,   *is coming*
gold leaves falling,   *to the country*
lipsticked coeds, sidelines full.

"Is there anything
you haven't done?" he asks.
Makes me smile.

In Yup'ik class—
"Nangerrluten!
Aqumluten nateqmun!
Palurrluten!"—
he lies down on the floor,
closes his eyes,   *coming*

and takes me
by surprise. This kid!
He brings things back—

how it feels to wake   *like a crown*
with a man   *of cranes*
and catch him

sleeping, dreaming,
gathering daylight.

Attraction

How the moon rises, almost full, giving sheen
    to the frozen slough
    and a human shadow, perhaps two,
    are seen walking or gliding through
    time and a mirror

How an ivory watchband comes to the wrist
    of the wearer, out of a black
    cold ocean alive with food:
    plankton, baleen,
    beluga whale

How the wearer carries spirits
    of ivory animals—polar bear, walrus, seal—
    and of food and the carver and the moon
    and the slough and skin drums
    and ice lace willows

How Raven circles the shadows
    as they glide and fall on the slough,
    laughing, getting up, laughing, falling, getting up again
    both fresh shadows
    skiing through

How some things attract,
    without intention,
    and nothing seems askew

After Reading
The Business of Fancydancing

Then a woman with bluish lips...
whispered in my ear:
"Can you describe this?"
And I answered: "Yes, I can."
—*Requiem,* Anna Ahkmatova

Because I wanted to teach college
Because I had taught in other schools
   for 17 years and had worked enough
   with remedial students
Because even the Yup'ik faculty members
   did not want to teach remedial courses
Because I did not want to be Director of Developmental Studies
Because *developmental* is a euphemism for *remedial*
   and the college in Bethel had been there for 20 years
   and the slogan on the commemorative T-shirts—
   "20 Years of Educational Excellence"—was a lie

Because I wanted to teach more than 10 of you
   without 2 or 3 absent each day
   and it was not my fault that one-third
   of the 25 members of your freshman class
   could not write or read at the 7th-grade level
Because I was not trained in remedial reading
   and I did not want to teach remedial reading
   I wanted to teach college
   and I did not like receiving anonymous letters
   that insisted I was racist

Because *A* means *Excellent*
    and a college student should be able to write and read

    but almost all of your semester grades
    in my classes were Cs and Ds
    and I had never had to give so many Cs and Ds
    and I did not deserve your anger and contempt
Because one of your favorite professors had said in a faculty meeting
    that I was "trying to put an iron gate around the college"
    I shook
    and could not comprehend
    this white professor, paid $70,000 a year (a kind man)
    who could not see a need for change
Because culture feeds
    the root of understanding
    but what right have whites to decide

    that Yup'iks do not need to know
    how to write and read?

Because I wanted to teach college
Because I could not continue
    to pour energy down a twisted hole
Because I loved you, but you could not feel it
Because there was too much to change and too little help,
    and $45,000 a year, comprehensive health insurance,
    and a generous retirement plan were not enough

Because my eyes were filled with blowing dust and tears
Because I, too, had a culture and a love for land

and I had no boat or small plane or snowmachine
just a need, sometimes, to drive away
I had patience, but not enough
I was not willing to wait, and wait, for change
I wanted to teach college
and I did not understand
politics
and I did not understand the grip
of money
I ached
Because I loved Yup'ik families
and I loved Bethel

but this job was dishonest
it was unethical
it was not college

and none would demand it

I want to come back
I will always come back
Because the Y-K Delta is one of my homes
and I am still learning from Yup'ik culture
and I am still learning from Yup'ik history

but my spirit
was dying
and I had never felt my spirit die
and I did not want my spirit to die

Because something much bigger than I
    was wrong

    and this thing
    was eating me up
    but I refused
    to be swallowed

    I swam away

Because I have been empowered to change my life
    Because I am white?
    Because I believe change is possible?

1992–2000

The Egg House in Bethel

Bumpy,
raven-pecked,
stuck on stilts
and stained
with soot and rusty water,
this foam dome
(which I rented)
sprouts
from tundra
like an egg
or a mushroom cap.
Ever facing east,
its white noggin
cocks a star-shaped eye
(my favorite),
while another eye
(up top, tall triangle) squints

with someone else's lamp
and hot pink curtain.

Fairbanks

Young girl in Bethel using a storyknife to draw the floor plan of a house while telling a story. Photographed by German ethnographer Hans Himmelheber, who visited parts of the Y-K Delta, including Bethel and Nunivak Island, in 1936–37.

Courtesy of Eberhard Fischer.
Photographer: Hans Himmelheber.

Lessons

So I drove home
and lit a fire in the woodstove
and sat on the blue rug
before the fire and the box

of kindling and the box
of logs, and I fed the fire
with birch and long sticks
of spruce I had split

on Christmas Day, and I thought
of the pretty blue bowls
on the shelf, the blue stoneware plates,
and the blue stained glass lamp

inside my cabin—this cabin
I have bought and made—
and of blue sky in summer
when a woman can sleep outdoors and dream

of waking with a man in the blue
dome tent. I fed the fire
with an occasional stick and with
my breath, blowing

on red coals the steady strength
of a flute-player's breath
and the lessons
of all those years.

I remembered silence.
I remembered listening.
I remembered longing.
People. Deep joy.

And I remembered tears.

I blew again
on the fire and I blew—
and blew and breathed and blew
and began, once more,

to thread a song.

When I Am 98

When I am 98
I want to remember
this: how I ran
inside the old college gym building
over arrows,
from the locker room,
down the hallway,
past the ski team bulletin board,
around the corner,
past the ROTC classroom
and the military posters—
Be All You Can Be,
Army ROTC Got Me the Job—
past the indoor rifle range, up the stairs,
down the hallway, past the weight room,
around the corner with mirrors,
past the hockey banner
and the basketball banner
and the vigorous young women
playing volleyball,
past the free telephone in its booth,
and the other weight room,
down the stairs, back to

the locker room, around
and around, up and down
stairs, again, down hallways,
over arrows (2 orange cones:
CAUTION—Runners Ahead)

my hand waving
at friends, my shoulders
passing other runners,
legs and arms pumping blood
and oxygen, drinking
the stale indoor air
of Fairbanks in winter, the shorter
steps of someone behind
pushing me to run
harder, faster, longer
strides, 1 for each of his 2,
my heart pumping, pumping, a laugh
escaping as he says from behind,
"You're too fast," and I stay ahead,
2 more laps around the hallways,
up and down stairs,
my black plastic watch
approaching 30 minutes, then
his gray head,
green running shorts,
pixie legs, Frank Williams,
Dean of Engineering,
passing at last,
        and I am alone,
again, still running, but slower,
catching my breath, remembering
this same oxygen debt
in races, how one runs

like a waterfall, like a fox
on the tundra, like there's no time
to lose, running
until my watch says 42.

And I want to remember
after, stretched out
like a corpse
on the thick, red-padded board
in the weight room,
AM rock music pulsing
on someone's boom box, the creaks
of weights and pulleys, men and women
pushing, lifting, grunting, and my body
long in a white T-shirt and shiny black tights,
tucking my Nike Air toes under the strap,
graywhitebrown hair wet, stuck
to the red board, how it feels
to close my eyes in this live room
and listen
                to a heartbeat,
                the brink of breath,
do 39 sit-ups,
then walk
down the dim
hallway, dizzy
with youth
and its thin
promises.

Notes of a Beautiful Woman
Living Alone

A moose ambles up the drive
past her small cabin, nibbles leaves.

Another moose jaywalks the road
near the foot of Chena Ridge.

Another moose charges three lanes of cars
and pickup trucks on Farmers Loop.

That evening at the Howling Dog,
a tall man asks to dance

and he is careful
with her fingers and her smile.

How she has come to notice
charms like these.

In pink midnight, a half moon rises
over all the heads.

At Ann's Greenhouse

Once upon a time there was a tall woman and a taller man. The tall woman's hair was turning white and the taller man's wasn't, but both the woman and the man showed wrinkles about their eyes when they smiled. This was because, even though they were both fast runners and not yet forty-five, like the flowers and the vegetable seedlings, already they were growing old.

The woman was always surprised to see the man (and sometimes, perhaps, the man was surprised to see the woman) when occasionally, in winter and in summer and in spring and in fall, their paths met. On this breezy Saturday afternoon, the woman was carrying a small cardboard box with four kinds of seedlings: one green citrosa to repel mosquitoes, twelve lobelia (blue, white, and lavender), one columbine, and six white daisies.

At the moment that the woman walked out of the greenhouse, looked up, and saw the man, all the flowers in the box burst into bloom. Like always, however, the man could not see them (nor did he want to, nor could she blame him, for she was growing old with white hair). She said, "Oh, hello. Did you come to buy flowers?" Even as she said this, she wished she could swallow it, for she knew what his answer would be. Did he ever buy flowers, she wondered, for anyone?

"Oh, no," he said. "I've come to buy vegetables." He looked down into her box, and this glance she found startling, even invasive, for usually he took no interest in her. She knew, however, that he could not see the blooms. He would never see the blooms, unless she launched them over his head. And even then, he might not see... Then what would she have lost?

They talked briefly in the shifting sun, both of them polite, as always, and frequently looking away. She made sure that she ended the conversation first, so that he could not make her feel more than she already did. "Well, see you later," she said, and he turned to seek vegetable seedlings.

She carried the box to her car and, without looking back, got in and drove away.

Later, walking to his parking place, the man did not notice the many little flower heads—blue, white, lavender—falling on his car.

Feeling and Knowing

She is standing on "her" land,
on her own two acres of land,
an October chinook kissing gently
the bare birch trees.

She has noticed, this darkening month,
how the Milky Way arches
directly overhead.

Tonight she is watching,
for the first time on her land, a band
of northern lights play the points
of the Milky Way. Offstage

fingers dance, white
and tickling the Dipper's bowl. A star
shoots through green—streak of silver—and she wishes

this might be enough.

The Nature of Prayer

Gather
the black nights, clear stars,
white moon rising
over a comforter of snow
and let it go, let it go

Listen
for geese and sandhill
cranes, their trails honking
on return
and let it go, let it go

Pretend
the days have not grown
longer, yellow midnight
pushing
into red

dawn wish
for a landing-place,
some sound of splashing, a signal
that this journey was not
in vain and

be ready
to receive a crack
a face
a spotted egg revealing
how to begin again

Leaving Alaska

I begin to understand
the reasons
I cannot seem to shake
this place
from the eye of my desire

it is a streaking sky

it is a thin birch

it is a bird song at night

and it is a fish, swimming   upriver,
reflecting light
safe return
the change of seasons
shiver of wind

and the white and black
moth that lands
like a Yup'ik word
on the triple-paned glass
of the cabin window
and tilts its patterned wings,
intricate and slim

marked

in the slanting sun
it flickers again

swimming
flicks again

Acknowledgements

The author gratefully acknowledges the following publications and other venues in which these poems first appeared:

AK (Alaska Public Radio Network weekly program): "Dr. Seuss & the Department of Fish & Game," "The Nature of Prayer"

Alaska Quarterly Review: "The Language Keepers," "Eskimo Dancing/*Yurarluni*"

Alaska Website Calendar: April: National Poetry Month (Alaska State Council on the Arts): "The Egg House in Bethel"

Anchorage Daily News: "The Nature of Prayer," "Feeling and Knowing"

Denali Alpenglow: "Backcountry Unit #12"

Fairbanks Daily News-Miner: "The Nature of Prayer," "Feeling and Knowing"

Field Notes: Friends of Creamer's Newsletter (Creamer's Field National Wildlife Refuge): "The Nature of Prayer"

Ice-Floe: International Poetry of the Far North: "Feeling and Knowing," "*Kass'aq* with Nunivak Mask," "Sestina Kyrie"

Ice Floe: New and Selected Poems (University of Alaska Press): "Sestina Kyrie"

The Last New Land: Stories of Alaska, Past and Present (Alaska Northwest Books): "At the Tetlin River," "Two with Spears"

Life on the Line: Selections on Words and Healing (Negative Capability Press): "The New Students"

Permafrost: "What Scares Me"

Place of the Pretend People: Gifts from a Yup'ik Eskimo Village (Alaska Northwest Books): "The Language Keepers," "The New Students," "The New Teacher"

poetryALASKAwomen: "Ancient Comb," "Sestina Kyrie"

Proceedings of the 8th World Wilderness Congress: "Leaving Alaska"

The Prose Poem: An International Journal: "Backcountry Unit #12"

Rock & Sling: "Sestina Kyrie"

Runner's World: "When I Am 98"

Steam Ticket: *A Third Coast Review*: "Bethel at Christmas"

The Tundra Drums: "At the Tetlin River," "Sestina Kyrie"

Wheelwatch Companion II: "The New Teacher"

A Whole Other Ballgame: Women's Literature on Women's Sport (Noonday Press): "When I Am 98"

1992 Year of Alaskan Poets Calendar: "Eskimo Dancing/*Yurarluni*"

Thanks to Seattle composer Lynette Westendorf for her musical setting of "Sestina Kyrie" for soprano, three percussionists, and three-person speaking chorus.

~

Sincere thanks, also, to the many people who helped this collection of words, images, pain, and wonder transform into a book.

In particular, *quyana* to James Barker, Dawn Biddison, Bodil Blum, Ann Fienup-Riordan, Eberhard Fischer, Peter Fux, Mareca Guthrie, Steve Henrikson, David Kingma, Angela Linn, Phyllis Morrow, Sara Piaseki, Monica Shah, Stephanie Summerhays, Lynn Ager Wallen, and R.T. Wallen for their invaluable help with photographs. My deep appreciation and thanks to Bruce Ford for his maps. *Quyana cakneq* to Joan Braddock, James Engelhardt, Sue Mitchell, Amy Simpson, and the University of Alaska Press for their generosity, patience, and creative work.

For their inspiration, encouragement, and suggestions, thank you to writers Marjorie Kowalski Cole, Joseph Enzweiler, John Haines, Christopher Howell, Holly Hughes, Jonathan Johnson, Oscar

Kawagley, John Keeble, Lisa Linsalata, Edna Ahgeak MacLean, E. Ethelbert Miller, N. Scott Momaday, John Morgan, Claire Rudolf Murphy, Harold Napolean, Richard "Nels" Nelson, Peggy Shumaker, Frank Soos, David Stark, Frank Stewart, Nance van Winckel, and Tom Walker. *Quyana* also to editors Marlene Blessing, Jessica Cochran, Elisabeth Dabney, Shannon Gramse, Sarah Kirk, and Suzanne Summerville.

For their friendship and longtime support of my writing and artistic efforts, thank you to Nelique Brons and family, Susan Campbell and Keith Echelmeyer, Lillian Corti, Linda Curda, Dorte Dissing and family, Susan Farnham, Sandy Gillespie, Jo Going, Kornelia Grabinska, Rolf Gradinger and family, Sarah Juday, Susanne and John Lyle, Dorli McWayne, Ben and Eliza Orr, Chris Pastro and family, Douglas Pfeiffer, Rob Quick, Tim Rains, Carol Scott, Mary Shields, Libby Silberling, Susan Todd, Sarah Trainor, Jill Wagner and family, Jessica Westfall, and many others unnamed.

Finally, *quyana* to the people of Tununak and the Yukon-Kuskokwim Delta for the inspiration and insights that your traditions, languages, and lifestyles continue to bring me. And thank you to my brother and sister, David Kremers and Nancy Kremers.

Life, like this book, is a pilgrimage—solitary, yet communal. *Quyana cakneq* to all and to the Earth.

Notes

smoothened   Village English for "smoothed"
Village English

Here is a definition from "Why Don't We Give Our Children to Our Native Languages?" by Edna Ahgeak MacLean (from a paper written for a class, School of Education, Stanford University, 1992, p. 4): "Out of the twenty languages indigenous to Alaska only two (Alaska Yupik and Siberian Yupik) are still spoken fluently by young children. Almost all of the Inuit and Athabaskan children speak English as their primary language of communication. Many of them understand some of their heritage language but cannot speak it. The English that they speak is usually influenced by the Native language spoken in their community. These varieties of English are called Village English in Alaska. They are dialects of English with many features of the local Native language embedded in their grammar and vocabulary. Perhaps more importantly, these dialects have as their communication base the discourse system of the local indigenous languages and cultures. Thus these varieties of English have the presentation of self, turn taking, organization of ideas and politeness strategies which are very different from those patterns of the standard English speaking teacher. Because of these differences, teachers often misunderstand students and determine that there is something wrong with the students' language."

circle-and-dot motif

In the Central Yup'ik language, this design is called *ellanguaq* (pretend or model world or universe). *Ellanguaq* also designates the wooden ring or rings sometimes placed around, or contained in, a Yup'ik dance mask.

80

Y-K   Yukon-Kuskokwim

Mamterillermiut
                 Original Yup'ik name, meaning Village of the People with
                 Many Fish Caches
yes, we change in this riverine town
                 In her article "Storyknifing: An Alaskan Eskimo Girls'
                 Game" (*Journal of the Folklore institute*, Indiana University,
                 March 1975, p. 192), cultural anthropologist Lynn Price
                 Ager made the following observations about storyknifing in
                 the Yukon-Kuskokwim Delta:
                 "There is more variety in the symbols used to represent
                 people than in any other aspect of the knifestory complex.
                 Each village has a different set of symbols (see Tables I
                 and II); however, locally one style commonly prevails, and
                 many girls seemed unaware that different symbols were
                 used elsewhere, unless they had had the opportunity to
                 travel. In some villages there are separate symbols for men,
                 women, children, old folks, dead people, sleeping people,
                 and so forth, while in other villages there might be only one
                 symbol used to represent any human being, whatever his
                 age, sex or condition...
                 In Bethel, one finds the greatest variety of character
                 symbols; this is probably due to the fact that Bethel is
                 a fairly large village to which many Eskimos have been
                 moving in recent years to find employment. The children
                 of Bethel, then, come from diverse communities, bringing
                 their own storyknifing styles with them."
tai-i-llu   and then

B.A.G.   Bethel Actors Guild

Nangerrluten!   Stand up!
Aqumluten nateqmun!
           Sit down on the floor!
Palurrluten!   Lie down on your stomach!

The Business of Fancydancing
           This is a collection of poems written by Sherman Alexie, Spokane/Coeur d'Alene Indian. First published in 1992, the book reflects life on the Spokane Indian Reservation. The pieces are honest, funny, irreverent, and human. Alexie speaks with the authority and freedom of an insider, a member of the tribe.

Requiem   *Requiem* is a long poem written between 1935 and 1961 by Russian poet Anna Akhmatova for herself, her imprisoned son, and her country. Censored in the Soviet Union, the poem was published in Munich in 1963 and first published in Russia in 1987.

           In his book *Eskimokünstler (Eskimo Artists)*, published in 1938 and translated into English in 1987, Hans Himmelheber wrote, "Eskimo women and girls down to the very smallest are passionate story-tellers [p. 28]. And they don't just narrate the stories, but combine them with two other arts: singing and drawing...It is scarcely imaginable how beloved this pastime is [p. 30]. On an almost dark, foggy cold night in Kukok around two o'clock I saw a woman telling stories to some girls on the shore. If they are unable to find comrades, the girls draw and narrate to themselves."

quyana cakneq
           thank you very much

Carolyn Kremers writes poetry and literary nonfiction and is a dedicated teacher and lifelong musician. Born in Denver, Colorado, and educated at Stanford and elsewhere, she moved to Alaska in 1986 to teach music and English in the village of Tununak. Later she completed a master of fine arts degree in creative writing and taught writing and literature to undergraduate and graduate students in Alaska and at Eastern Washington University in Spokane. She designed and implemented the MFA literary nonfiction program at Eastern. Currently she teaches part-time at the University of Alaska Fairbanks.

Kremers's other books include the memoir *Place of the Pretend People: Gifts from a Yup'ik Eskimo Village* and *The Alaska Reader: Voices from the North*, an anthology of fiction, nonfiction, poetry, and oral tradition co-edited with Anne Hanley. *Upriver* is a sequel to *Place of the Pretend People*.

Poems and essays by Kremers have appeared in numerous journals, magazines, and anthologies, as well as on the Internet and public radio. She has been artist-in-residence at Gates of the Arctic National Park and at Denali National Park, and she is a founding member of the Alaska artists and scientists group, In a Time of Change. In 2008–2009, she was a US Fulbright Scholar at Buryat State University in Ulan Ude, Russia. Kremers lives at the edge of Fairbanks in a log cabin surrounded by birch trees and spends as much time as possible outdoors.